THE REAL DIRT ON
COMPOSTING

ALSO BY CHERYL WILFONG

THE REAL DIRT ON
COMPOSTING

CHERYL WILFONG

H𝒫

Cheryl Wilfong
Heart Path Press, L3C
314 Partridge Road
Putney VT 05346

www.meditativegardener.com

The Real Dirt on Composting

Book design and illustrations by Carolyn Kasper
Cover photo: iStock

ISBN: 978-0-9825664-7-3

Follow The Meditative Gardener *on Facebook*

CONTENTS

THE INS & OUTS OF COMPOST COMPOSITION: GREENS & BROWNS 33

THE REALITY OF COMPOSTING 61

CRITTERS   87

USING YOUR COMPOST 97

THE PHILOSOPHY OF COMPOSTING 111

WHY COMPOST?

WHY COMPOST?

W E KNOW INTUITIVELY THAT compost is good for us, good for our gardens, and good for our planet. We can join the green planet movement by traveling no farther than our own backyards.

Let's make our very own compost: that rich, dark brown, crumbly humus that sustains our houseplants, flowerbeds, and vegetable gardens. Compost nourishes the cherry tomato on the patio as well as the lettuces, beans, and broccoli growing in our gardens, which in turn nourish us.

Stroll with me on a journey through the ins and outs of composting. Turn your kitchen scraps and yard waste into what composters call "black gold." You can send a wealth of nutrients downstream, or you can send them to your garden. It's your choice. You can treat your compost like trash and haul it to the landfill. Or you can fill your own land with the same nutritious food you and your family eat, and thereby create a haul of treasure. It's as easy as feeding your family, and then feeding the leftovers—your "post-consumer waste"—to your garden.

Composting ties us into the web of life. We pitch our dead plants onto the pile, and the following spring, new life springs up. Compost is a miracle. Our garden is a miracle, and our planet, well, it's a miracle too. Now, let's start growing green miracles with our very own compost.

COMPOST: WHY BOTHER?

WHY BOTHER MAKING YOUR own compost when you can go to the garden center and buy a 40-quart bag for $7.99?

Some of us are do-it-yourselfers—we'd rather save money and spend time. And some of us shoppers would rather save time and just spend the money.

But are we really saving time when we buy compost at the garden center? We have to remember that driving to the garden center and back takes how long? Half an hour plus another fifteen or so minutes to buy the bag of compost. You've spent nearly an hour in your car and in the store. I'd rather "spend" that hour in the garden, myself. Besides, we have to *spend* time at work in order to earn the money to *buy* the compost.

So the do-it-yourselfer saves money and "saves" time and "spends" her time in the garden. The shopper spends her money and time at the garden center, which is so full of other beautiful and tempting things to buy as well.

The shopper winds up with several plastic bags, and how do you reuse or recycle plastic bags anyway? The do-it-yourselfer is plastic-bag-free.

What is it that we truly desire? More stuff? Or more happiness? Stuff seems to make us happy, for a few minutes anyway. We all do truly desire happiness. We just have different ways of searching for it.

My happiness is in the garden with the birds singing all around me. My happiness is hauling my hand-made compost to my vegetable garden. My happiness is planting a seed. My happiness is watching life and death unfold all around me in the garden where I am having the time of my life.

MY COMPOST SITUATION

As a MASTER GARDENER and Master Composter, people often ask me about compost. My short answer is "Time." Compost takes time. My next shortest answer is "It depends." It depends on your situation.

Here's mine: I live in a rural area, sharing my land with many wild creatures and some neighborhood dogs. My closest neighbor is a hundred yards away, hidden in the woods. All my neighbors have compost piles in various states of use and disuse. Compost seems like a good idea, but commitment wavers and varies.

My home is in Vermont, which has four strong seasons—a short and sometimes buggy lettuce-green spring followed by a humid Green-Mountain-green summer, a spectacular red-orange-yellow autumn, and a white and cold winter that lasts from Thanksgiving to spring equinox.

Native New Englanders like to say we have two additional seasons: at the end of winter, we have mud season when the snow melts but the ground is still frozen, and there's nowhere for the spring run-off to go. And before winter begins, we have November—a month of tain't season, when it tain't autumn (the leaves have fallen) but tain't winter either because the snow hasn't fallen.

Perhaps tain't season has the most to teach us about compost because our own compost can seem like "tain't compost" for quite a long while.

The effect of these seasons on my compost piles is that in the spring, I'm busy dividing plants and giving away baby plants in containers of pure, rich compost. Summer is a good time for projects—for ripping out overgrown beds and piling cartloads of greenery onto the compost pile. In the fall, I heap on brown leaves and garden clean-up. Then winter freezes my compost into an iceberg, which eventually thaws sometime in April.

If you are looking for a hot compost pile that steams all winter and has dozens of wriggling worms in the summer, that is not my compost pile. My compost is ordinary. And yet it is extraordinary in that everything decomposes in time. Decomposes into beautiful, rich compost.

Your situation will be different from mine, yet your compost too will take time. Perhaps lots of time. While your compost is resting, rest your mind. Your compost isn't worrying, and you don't need to worry either. Life is unfolding and the lessons of life are awaiting us there in our very own compost pile.

SETTING UP YOUR COMPOST

THE MORE BINS, THE BETTER

W HAT'S THE BEST METHOD of composting? "It depends" is the answer.

If you live in town, then you probably want one of those black plastic units. Our landfill sells them for a cheaper price than you can buy them in the catalog, either by mail or online. Check out your landfill's website. While you're at it, buy two composters, so you can add to one while the other is "resting." Otherwise, you suffer the frustration of trying to ladle out a trowelful of compost from the underside of a digesting plastic belly.

If you live in bear country (and there are more and more reports of bears near houses), then you want a really big, heavy, black plastic unit that the lid screws onto. The bears may roll it away, but they (hopefully) won't be able to get into it.

I live in the countryside, so I have three open bins—each made of four wooden pallets, which are set upright to form a square and simply tied together with rope at each corner. E-Z. These bins can be assembled in ten minutes and disassembled in five. A local company, which uses a lot of paper products, always has a pile of pallets to give away. Once a year, I drive my truck over there and load up, because pallets are easy-to-assemble compost bins in disguise.

I line up the three bins beside each other—one I am "adding to"; one is resting; and one I am "subtracting from," using the cooked compost to pot up plants or to scatter on various garden beds.

I add to the newest one pile every day—garbage and leaves, flower deadheads and garden trimmings. The middle-aged pile was topped off last fall with a layer of manure from the local dairy farm. It just sits there, resting and digesting, under an accumulation of last fall's leaves.

The third pile—the one that I'm subtracting from—collected a winter's cap of leaves to keep itself warm, but in the spring, I rake it clean and toss the leaves into the neighboring "add to" bin. Having removed the skim of leaves, I finally see the sunken heap, only half as high as it was in the fall. Dead leaves, dead flowers, and garbage have all been miraculously transformed into living soil. This pile is the one I dig into almost every day, especially in the spring—using its rich black humus when I transplant plants or pot up extra plants I find volunteering in places where I don't want them.

When the "subtract from" bin is totally empty, the pallets that surrounded it look quite decrepit. After two or three years of containing compost, the pallets themselves have also rotted. I haul them off to a brush pile and erect new pallets. Now, the empty bin becomes the new "add to" pile, the old "resting" heap becomes the "subtract from" pile, and the former "add to" agglomeration can now "rest."

All this adding to and subtracting from "adds up" to beautiful compost for the garden.

HOW TO USE A BLACK
PLASTIC COMPOSTER

BLACK PLASTIC COMPOST BINS and tumblers are great for collecting and containing kitchen scraps, and they are good at keeping smells and critters away, to some extent, but they're not so good at producing finished compost.

The tumblers are meant to spare us the arduous task of turning the pile. Just rotate the composter, which is balanced on a frame. But the tumblers can be heavy to turn and it becomes a chore that no one wants to do.

As regards the free-standing units, you can dig a few trowelfuls of compost out of the bottom. Then you run the risk of the garbage inside collapsing down into the space you've emptied out, and that's the end of your compost collection.

A black plastic composter is a finicky eater. It is built to digest kitchen scraps with some dead leaves or maybe a bit of hay for balance. Throw in a shovelful of dirt occasionally to add micro-organisms.

Since the diet of a black plastic composter is somewhat restricted, you can collect many of the things you would otherwise throw into a compost bin: paper napkins, paper towels, and pizza boxes—and take them to the composting program at your landfill. Because orange peels and grapefruit rinds and eggshells take a long time to decompose in a composter, you can also take those.

Some persistent critters do try to burrow into the composter from the bottom. And it will take less than a week for raccoons to figure out how to take off the lid, if there is one. Dogs can also tear off the lid.

A black plastic composter is a good way to get started composting. It's like composting with training wheels. Then once you have your composting routine established, you'll better know your needs and be able to customize your personal compost system. For those in suburban areas, the black plastic composter may be your only option.

If you outgrow your composter, you can use it as a storage bin rather than for actual composting. You can store your raw garbage in the composter during the winter when very little composting is actually happening. Or you can store your finished compost in the composter so the nutrients won't leach out.

Start your composting life cycle with a black plastic composter and pretty soon, you'll take off the training wheels and be offering free-wheeling compost advice to your friends and neighbors.

SOMETIMES A BLACK PLASTIC COMPOSTER IS YOUR ONLY OPTION

I F YOU LIVE IN town or in the city, you have several other people or neighbors to satisfy about this composting business. A black plastic composter looks neat, contains smells, and gives the illusion of keeping critters out. These benefits should satisfy your neighbors' or your spouse's doubts about composting.

Although composting is an easy-to-take step on our path of saving the earth, a compost pile can generate a lot of not-in-my-back-yard (NIMBY) and not-in-your-backyard-either sentiment.

Composting saves our town's tax dollars by keeping organic waste out of the landfill. Forty percent of town trash is organic waste that could be composted. And, of course, creating a new landfill when the current one is filled up generates its own share of NIMBY.

So, when sensitive neighbors are nearby, a black plastic composter works well. It looks neat and tidy and keeps the mess of compost out of their sight and scent.

RECYCLED COMPOST BINS

Mary Lou believes in recycling whatever she has on hand rather than going out and buying something new.* Her husband is a contractor, so she constructed her compost bins out of cinder blocks, held in place with a metal fence post in every other block, to prevent them from collapsing.

She divided this ten-foot long U-shaped bin into three sections by salvaging some corrugated translucent fiberglass roofing panels left over from a cold frame. Sections of metal roofing work just as well. The panels are held in place by more metal fence posts.

Here's how Mary Lou's three-bin system works: She adds to the bin on the left. The middle bin "rests." The bin on the right is "finished." When the "finished" bin is empty or when the first "receiving" bin is full, whichever comes first, she forks the middle bin into the third, then forks the first into the middle.

Mary Lou has a big house and a small yard in town. Her upstairs tenant and a couple of friends contribute

* Freecycle.org is an excellent way to find free materials near you. Join your city or regional freecycle and post your requests for whatever you have to give away or whatever materials you might be searching for.

their kitchen scraps to her compost bin too. Mary Lou not only recycles found materials, she also recycles her friends' materials.

Are there materials in your yard or garage that you can use to build compost bins? You might even have some neighbors who could contribute to your compost.

INDISPENSABLE
COMPOST EQUIPMENT

ABSOLUTELY NECESSARY FOR COMPOSTING is a compost bucket sitting beside your sink in the kitchen.

My mother used to have a triangular garbage strainer sitting in the corner of our porcelain kitchen sink. A colander would work just as well.

Nowadays, you can buy a purpose-built little compost bucket with a lid. I bought a ceramic cookie jar 20 years ago. The lid was broken soon afterward, so my kitchen compost is lid-less. Since we take it out every day, smell is not an issue. The cookie jar "look" hides the garbage contents, so visitors to my home have a hard time finding the compost, even though they're looking for it, and it's right in front of their nose.

I found a plastic container with a wide mouth (baby wipes, if you must know) that fits perfectly inside this compost/cookie jar. This "insert" is easy to carry back and forth to the compost bin and to wash out.

Five-gallon buckets are the handmaidens of any gardener. For a while, I coasted along on buckets left over from a construction project. Then I found some buckets at a garage sale. Then I actually had to buy my next generation of buckets at the farm and garden supply store. I found them in the horse department.

Stroll through your garden with clippers in one hand and a bucket in the other. Clip off deadheads, cut down old stems, pick up leaves, and throw them in the bucket. Carrying the bucket to the compost bin constitutes gardener's exercise. Instead of weights, we use buckets for much more interesting repetitions.

I love my garden cart. Mine is 48 inches long by 29 inches wide by 18 inches high. Buy a smaller one as opposed to a larger one. Really now, how much heavy stuff do you want to haul?

I prefer the two-wheeled garden cart to a wheelbarrow, partly for balance, partly for volume, and partly because you can lift out the front panel and slide any number of heavy items—garden statues or shrubs—into the cart. After you've lifted a sheaf of yard and garden waste into the compost, you can easily tip up the cart and let the dirt crumbs slide out. That's what I call E-Z cleaning.

From summer solstice until fall equinox, the garden cart can be counted on to haul volumes of gone-by perennials, weeds (pre-seed, hopefully), and rotten vegetables to the compost pile.

Little by little or lot by lot, we just keep adding to our compost pile.

COMPOST PARAPHERNALIA

I THINK I'VE BOUGHT EVERY single piece of compost paraphernalia in the catalog:

1. a black plastic composter
2. a compost aerator (a giant corkscrew)
3. a compost activator
4. a compost thermometer
5. a sifter
6. a leaf shredder
7. a compost bin cover

After all that shopping, I don't use any of these compost gadgets.

When I realized that the bottom outlet of the black plastic unit was only big enough for a trowel, and I need shovelfuls of compost, I put the composter on the sidewalk with a sign that said "Free." It was gone in 15 minutes.

The compost aerator. Well, I just never found the time to stand at the compost pile and twist the big corkscrew into it. After seven years of seeing the aerator lolly gagging around the compost bins, I finally took it to the

Swap Program at the landfill. My trash is now someone else's treasure.

A compost activator is a waste of money. Micro-organisms already exist in your kitchen scraps and in your dirt. They will activate your compost just as well as something from a bag or a jar. Just shovel a scoop of dirt on your pile and voila! The vast numbers of micro-organisms that are in the dirt, and maybe worms too, are now in your compost pile. You also can read the label of the compost activator to find out what's so active about the "activator." You can buy the ingredients, such as blood meal and bone meal, at your garden supply store.

I never even tried my compost thermometer because it was pretty obvious that my compost pile was frozen in the winter. The summer temperature was the same inside the pile as out.

The sifter also hangs around the compost pile. I use it a few times a year when I need fine compost to add to potting soil.

Yes, I actually bought a used leaf shredder and used it once. Since I do not relish dealing with mechanical equipment, I sold it on Craigslist two years later, and, fortunately, broke even.

A compost bin cover. What was I thinking? I have a roll of black plastic sitting in my basement that I can cut to size and use the resulting square sheet of plastic to cover my finished compost.

Oh, those compost gadgets are so enticing. They're so beautiful when they're new. Enthusiasm and my credit card carry me away. The next thing you know, I'm older and wiser.

And my compost pile just carries on and does its own thing. Despite all those gadgets, garbage turns itself into compost.

TRENCH COMPOSTING

WE ALL LEARNED ABOUT composting in grade
school when we read that Squanto saved the Pil-
grims by teaching them to plant a dead fish under each
hill of corn. I have, myself, planted the occasional dead
fish from my fishpond next to a nearby perennial.

Nowadays, Squanto's technique is called the trench
method. Dig a trench twelve inches deep in an unused
section of your garden. Every day, bury your compostables
in the trench and cover them up with dirt. You can even
bury your weeds.

The so-called "trench" can be any shape, whatever
makes sense to you in your situation—long or short,
circular or rectangular. Design your own trench.

With the trench method, you don't have to worry
about compost composition, turning the compost pile,
or moving it from one place to another. Simply cover
the kitchen scraps, the weeds, or what have you, and you
are done. In as little as one month, your compost will be
ready and waiting right where the roots of your plants
need it—several inches underground.

The trench method deals with concerns about varmints and odors by burying your kitchen scraps directly

into your vegetable garden. And it's invisible, so you can compost even if you live in an area that doesn't "allow" composting.

If trench composting fits your situation, don't squander this opportunity to compost.

PROJECT COW
(Composting Organic Waste)

O UR LOCAL LANDFILL HAS a composting program they call Project COW. Because they are dealing with large volumes of waste, they can take things that you would not ordinarily add to your compost at home.

ALL FOOD WASTES	NON-RECYCLABLE PAPER
Cooked or Raw Meat, Fish & Shellfish	Soiled or Waxed Cardboard
Fruits/Vegetables & Peelings	Milk & Juice Cartons (please remove plastic spouts)
Cheese and Other Dairy Products	Damp/Wet Paper
Coffee Grounds, Paper Filters & Tea Bags	Paper Towels, Tissues & Napkins
Bread/Rice/Pasta/Beans	Paper Plates & Cups
Eggshells	Frozen Food Boxes (wax coated only)
Cooking Oils & Fats	Soiled Pizza Boxes
Pet Wastes or Bedding	Cardboard Egg Cartons
Garden Weeds	Sugar or Flour Bags (without plastic liners)

Many towns and cities now require curbside composting. This means they are creating tons of compost at the landfill. You can contribute to this effort by keeping a small Rubbermaid box or a plastic bucket in an out-of-the-way spot in the kitchen or utility room and throwing in your compostables. No sorting. People who live in neighboring towns can bring their scraps directly to the landfill.

Project COW does not take yard debris. Your leaves, grass clippings, and brush have to go elsewhere.

Because a town can generate a mountain of compost, the heat in the pile will literally cook everything in the pile at a much higher temperature than you ever could at home. When you're ready for finished compost for your garden, you can buy a truckload for $20 or bring your bucket and fill it for $5.

Let the town do your composting for you.

HIDDEN IN PLAIN VIEW

YOUR COMPOST PILE NEEDS to be handy and easily accessible; otherwise, you won't go there. If you want to actually use your compost bin, situate it close to a path you regularly travel. The corollary to "easily accessible" is: *Hide it in plain view.*

My driveway is bordered by trees and shrubs. The house is straight ahead, and that's where the eye travels to. A parking area is off to the left, and that's where my three compost bins are hiding behind a forsythia bush. I usually park my car in front of the bins.

When visitors turn into the driveway, they see the house with eye-popping magenta trim. They see an arbor beckoning them into the garden beyond. Their peripheral vision may register a green bush and a blue car, but not the compost bins that are ten feet from where they park their car.

These focal points of house, arbor, and garden distract the visitor's eye. In fact, many people don't even see that there's a parking area for their car, right beside my car! Instead they park in front of the garage door.

When they get out of their car, they are looking at the gardens or the front door, and not at those camouflaged compost bins behind them. In the summer, I further disguise the bins with morning glories growing over the compost bin fencing.

You also want your compost bin to be accessible in winter. For those of us in the North Country, this means placing it within a few, and I mean a very few, feet of your snowplowed driveway. You don't want to wade through knee-deep snow; you do not want to snowshoe to your compost pile; neither do you want to snow-shovel it. My compost pile is eighteen inches from the driveway. In the winter, that's a mere two shovelfuls of snow.

Every day, when I walk out to my car, my sweetie reminds me to take out the little kitchen bucket full of compost. Maybe that compost pile is *too* handy?

COMPOST CAMOUFLAGE

IN JULY, MY COMPOST bins are camouflaged with morning glory vines growing all over them. In fact, the compost bin is so well camouflaged (okay, you can call it overgrown), that a guest could not see it even though it was literally right in front of her eyes and right beside where she parked her car.

We are so distracted by beauty (of the purple morning glory flowers) or so repelled by ugliness (the weediness of the overgrown compost bin), or just plain oblivious (*What? Where's the compost pile?*), that we fail to notice the cycle of life that's right in front of our eyes.

Beautiful life is growing out of garbage and yard debris. Amazing, isn't it?

BACKSTAGE IN THE GARDEN

W<small>HEN</small> I <small>VISIT A</small> garden, I'm always on the lookout for where the owner hides her inventory. Every beautiful garden has a backstage area, and I want to see it. Where does she hide the compost? The brush pile? The heaps of wood chips or bark mulch? Where does she put the dead plants? Does she pot up her divided plants? How does she camouflage the inner workings of the garden?

I like being on this treasure hunt. Where are the tools of the trade located? The shovels, the flower pots, the clippers and loppers? Where do people keep the stuff that makes the garden beautiful?

The set and the scenery of the garden itself may be fantastic, but more than garden gnomes are at work. Real people have been sweating, digging, and hauling, although by the time I arrive, their tracks have been covered, the walks have been swept, and all is calm.

Sometimes the storage area is beautiful too. (Although that's nearly beyond my personal comprehension.) Some gardeners actually do find a place for everything, and put everything in its place. But, more often, behind the scenes looks not unlike the back staging area of my garden—heaps of unused or disused garden materiel.

Then I stroll back into the garden, content, and am greeted the garden's owner in her clean clothes and clogs.

THE INS & OUTS OF COMPOST COMPOSITION: GREENS & BROWNS

THE CARE AND TENDING
OF COMPOST BINS

THE EXPERTS SAY YOU should layer your compost with equal amounts of green and brown; you should turn your compost; and you should chop your compost into bits and pieces.

But my compost pile is not the focus of my life. I want to be good to the environment and good to my garden, but I also want to be good to my back. I am never going to be turning over my compost pile with a pitchfork. I don't have a spare teenager around the house whom I can send outdoors with a shovel to work off some steam. I am not going to be putting my compost on a cutting board and slicing and dicing (or hacking and thwacking) like Julia Child. I just don't have that kind of time in my life. And I don't expect you do either.

Instead, I do my best at layering the green and the brown as I go along. In the spring and the summer, there's a lot of green. In the fall, there's a lot of brown. Sigh. The "layers" are thicker (way thicker) than what the university extension service recommends.

I do make an extra effort to add a lot of green. Rhubarb leaves are excellent for this purpose, and so are carrot tops. Dividing the plants in your perennial garden, as hard as it is, and tossing the extras into the compost is another excellent source of green.

Manure *used to be* green grass growing in a pasture, and then our four-footed friends ate it. So manure is "green," even though it looks brown.

I add a big slug of manure to the bins at any time of the year when I have the inclination or the time or the truck. But definitely in November, I pick up a load of manure at the local farm and use it to "top off" three bins of compost that have already reached the brim with fall clean-up. Then they can sit and "cook" all winter.

Since you and I are not turning, watering, or chopping up our compost, the actual decomposing of the compost will take longer. We are simmering our compost, not roasting it. Therefore, it won't cook as fast as the gourmet compost. But both varieties will "taste" the same to the garden.

Let that heap simmer in its own juices for a year or two. Don't rush it. Just simmer down, my friend. In order to "tenderize" our compost, we are tending it by being tender to it and to ourselves.

FOOD PYRAMID

THE HEALTHY EATING FOOD Pyramid recommends three or more servings of vegetables every day plus two or three servings of fruit. We can serve the same balance to our compost pile: more or less equal servings of green, leafy vegetables balanced with the carbohydrates of sweet fruit plus the high fiber of woody stalks and stems. A plant-based diet is healthiest not only for us, but for our compost pile as well.

The Healthy Eating Pyramid encourages us to eat a balanced diet for the well-being of our bodies. Our compost pile also works best if it has a balanced diet of green vegetables and leaves (nitrogen) and brown fiber (carbohydrates in the form of carbon).

RECIPE FOR COMPOST

W**HAT'S YOUR RECIPE FOR** compost?" a friend asks. Oh dear. I compost like I cook.

After looking at a recipe—half green / half brown—I make a lot of substitutions and add a few ingredients that aren't in the original recipe. The result is a delicious mixture of rich, dark brown, crumbly compost.

It looks good enough for the plants to eat.

For those who like to follow a recipe exactly, here's the compost scoop:

If you are composting in a black plastic bin and using mainly kitchen scraps, add a handful of scrunched-up dead leaves every time you empty your kitchen pail into the black plastic bin. The leaves (brown) will balance the "green" of the kitchen scraps.

If you have a heap where you throw all your grass clippings, garden excess, and yard debris, but you <u>don't</u> use kitchen scraps for fear of varmints, then do not add woody stalks and stems or dead leaves. The flower stalks and stems will overload the pile with brown, resulting in a dry, "constipated" pile.

If you add wheelbarrow-loads of garden detritus to your pile every day or every week, you'll have large amounts of green going into your pile during the summer and large amounts of brown going in during fall clean-up. My rule of the green thumb for this situation is: Add more green. Think rhubarb leaves, comfrey, or horseradish leaves. Maybe it's time to rip out a ground cover or divide some of those seriously overgrown perennials. Your compost pile is hungry for more vegetation, more vegetable matter.

The recipe says the proper temperature for cooking compost is 140 degrees. I do not know a single person whose compost reaches this temperature. In fact, if your compost pile is smaller than a cube three feet on each side, you are doomed to cool compost. So, let's pretend we are part of the raw food movement, which recommends not cooking your food at more than 105 degrees, such as the hottest day of summer. Our compost will only simmer; it will not steam. Still, our little, cool, slow-cooking pile will be creating lovely delicious compost for our garden.

Cooking time varies widely. You can probably extract a wheelbarrow load of compost out of your black plastic unit every spring. Last summer's grass clippings pile will be ready the following spring.

Even though the recipe for compost piles and bins says four to six months, my recommendation is to set your timer for two or three years, because time will cure whatever shortcomings your pile may have.

We don't have to bake our compost to perfection. We are not taking our compost to the county fair bake-off. We just want good-enough compost to feed our plant children. Children like the way their mother cooks food, and our plants will enjoy whatever compost we cook up for them.

COMPOST ALPHABET

Green = Nitrogen	Brown = Carbon (& Carbohydrates)	No-No's
Apple cores	Avocado shells & pits	*Ashes*
Banana skins	Brown paper bags	*Bones*
Coffee grounds in filters	Corncobs	*Charcoal*
Daffodil deadheads	Dried fruit	*Dairy products*
Eggshells	Egg cartons (shredded)	*E-coli (fresh cow pies)*
Feathers	Flour products, fruitcake	*Fat*
Grass clippings	Gummy bears	*Grease (e.g., bacon)*
Horseradish leaves	Halloween candy, Hay	*Herbicide-treated weeds*
Iceberg lettuce	Icing	*Ice cream*
Juice pulp	Jellybeans (sugar)	*Junket*
Kiwi skins	Ketchup	*Kefir*
Lettuce leaves	Leaves	*Lint (synthetic fibers)*
Manure (herbivores)	Muffins	*Meat*
Nasturtium leaves	Newspaper (shredded)	*Needles, pine*
Orange rinds	Onion skins	*Oils*
Pumpkin	Paper, paper towels	*Pet poop*
Quinoa	Quantity = 40-50%	*Quilts*
Rhubarb leaves	Raffia	*Rugs (synthetic fibers)*
Seaweed (wash salt off)	Stalks & stems, straw	*Sawdust (too acidic)*
Tea bags	Toilet paper tubes	*Thistles (spread by root)*
Urine	Used napkins, tissues Underpants (cotton)	*Urethane*
Vegetables	Vacuum dust (no synthetic rug fibers though)	*Velvet and velour (synthetics)*
Watermelon rinds	Wool	*Weeds with seeds or roots that spread by rhizome*
Xanthorhizus (yellow root)	Xerox paper	*X This No-No List*
Yams	Yard debris (chopped up)	*Yogurt*
Zucchini	Zwieback	*Zippers*

THE INS AND OUTS OF COMPOST

I TAKE EVERY OPPORTUNITY TO educate people about the ins and outs of compost: what goes in—the greens (i.e., nitrogen) and the browns (i.e., carbon) and what stays out—wood ash, meat scraps, dairy, and fats.

What I usually don't talk about are all the random things I smuggle in when nobody's looking.

coffee filters
used tissues
paper towels that have
    had food on them
tea bags
paper napkins
toilet paper rolls
twisty ties (not the
    plastic ones)
dryer lint

candy
used matches
Q-tips (not the
    plastic ones)
waxed paper
cellophane
hair from my hairbrush
fingernail and toenail
    clippings
Christmas wreath

One of the reasons we are composting is to cut down on what we send to our local (or not so local) landfill. Inch by inch we are saving space in our landfills, and drop by drop we are saving the fossil fuel needed to transport trash from our driveway to the landfill in one of those giant trash trucks. One by one we are slowly cutting down on the number of plastic bags we haul out to the end of the driveway.

And to top it off, we are growing dinner from our compost. Now that's a real trash-to-treasures story.

NO WEEDS, PLEASE

O H, IT IS SO tempting to toss the weeds into the compost pile. But don't do it! You're just recycling weeds.

This means you need an easy alternative. Where are you going to put your weeds?

In the spring, I do throw weeds into my compost with this caveat: *They aren't blooming, and they have not set seed yet.* Some grasses don't set seed until late summer, so I can toss their greenery into the compost until then.

But once a weed is flowering (and some of them have tricky green flowers) or definitely when a weed has gone to seed, here are some possibilities:

Throw weeds into the woods. I live in the country, so I can throw my weeds into the woods. *Good luck growing in the shade,* I think as I toss them into the trees.

Create a dry-and-die pile. Set out a square of black plastic or a black trash bag and put your weeds onto it. On a sunny day, they'll bake to death in just a few hours. Perhaps even cover them loosely with the black plastic so they'll double bake in the sun. A day or two later, you can add your sun-dried weeds to your trash, where they'll take up a lot less space (and weigh less) than when they were green. And they'll create a lot less methane once they are in the landfill.

I live in an area where burning is permitted, so I throw my dried weeds onto a brush pile. If you have a fire pit, pitch them in there.

Another version of the dry-and-die pile is to use a bucket or a trug that you won't need for the foreseeable future. I have one invasive weed that I call Enemy. Enemy can gallop through a flowerbed in no time. And here is its secret: It grows from the tiniest rootlet left in the ground. I definitely do not want to spread Enemy around, so I carefully put it and all the roots I can find into a bucket. If I only have one bucketful, I cremate it in the wood stove. But if I have a trug-ful, I let them molder until it's time for my next campfire.

After all, we don't want s'more weeds.

SHOULD YOU COMPOST ASHES?

Those of us with wood-burning stoves would love to put those wood ashes into the compost. It seems like such a natural place to dispose of ashes, yet all compost advice says "no ashes." (Okay. We sneak some in anyway.)

Here's why we do *not* add ashes to our compost: Ashes are alkaline. They're good for the acidic soils of the Northeast U.S. and places that receive acid rain, but they're too powerful for compost. Wood ashes soaked in rainwater for three days become lye, a caustic potash. We don't want the ashes in our compost to convert to lye and kill the microbes.

We add compost to our gardens in the spring, and lime (or ashes) in the fall, due to slow absorption. The problem with this scenario is that we don't have ashes in the fall. We have ashes in the winter and spring. Sprinkle those ashes directly on your lawn or flowerbeds or on the snow covering them. Ashes are excellent for melting ice, but remove your shoes at the door if you don't want ash tracks throughout the house.

Areas with alkaline soils have absolutely no need for

alkaline wood ashes. One possible exception is to kill viral weeds with extremely pH so that nothing will grow on the site where the wood ashes are applied.

We want our plants to grow, but we don't want to overpower them with too much of a good thing or they may not rise from the ashes next spring.

CONSTIPATED COMPOST

Y OU KNOW WHAT NOT enough water in your diet leads to: constipation. Your compost pile can get constipated with too many stalks, stems, and dead plants. In composter-ese, this impacted condition is called "too much brown."

Dousing your pile with water might help, but it can also lead to compost diarrhea—a very unpleasant gooey mess with attendant icky smells.

Eating too much candy (carbohydrates) can give you a bellyache, and too much carbon (brown stuff) can give your compost pile a bellyache.

The remedy for dry and scratchy compost is to add more vegetable matter, more green, into the diet of your compost pile. Kitchen scraps are an easy solution, unless you are concerned about varmints. The suburban gardener can add grass clippings (if the lawn has not been treated with chemicals). Add big green leaves such as rhubarb leaves, squash leaves, carrot tops, or bolted lettuce. If you're not getting around to eating your kale and collards, add those. They're as good for the digestive health of your compost as they are for you. Manure will also solve the blockage.

In any case, it will probably take a few months for your compost pile to relax its cramped belly. Be patient with your sickly (or stick-ly) compost. It just needs to get some rest. Continue feeding your compost healthy doses of greens while you wait for the indigestion to run its course. Time heals all.

SWEET AND SALTY COMPOST

A NOTHER THING I THROW into the compost pile is candy. Halloween candy. Christmas candy (or fruitcake). Easter candy. Whenever I find myself with too much of a good sweet thing, I pitch it onto the compost pile in order to lead myself out of temptation.

Chips are actually the tantalizing treat that I crave. If I buy the 99-cent bag (such a good deal!) while I'm on a long drive, I pitch the remains of my salty treat into the compost bin when I get home. You may wonder how long it would take me to realize the 99 cents wasn't that great a deal if I was throwing half the bag away: years. It took years, but I finally started buying the lunch-bag size of chips. Fewer chips and fewer calories. Less temptation and less compost.

Consider composting the treats you know are not really good for you, and be good to your garden instead. The earth can handle some things better than we can.

LOBSTER-SHELL COMPOST

FRIENDS WHO RENT A summer house in Maine come home with a five-gallon bucket full of lobster shells. They've already taken a shovel and crunched the lobster shells into bits in order to compact them. (There are a lot of lobsters in Maine!) When they arrive home, they dump the pulverized lobster shells onto the compost pile.

The main component of crustacean exoskeletons is chitin, which can improve overall crop yields by building strong cell walls. Strong lobster shells make strong plant cells. Chitin also induces defense mechanisms in plants, strengthening their immune system to diseases.

Yes, my Maine friends do occasionally find bits of red lobster shell in their garden, but eventually it breaks down.

Well composted lobster shell makes your garden prosper well.

SEAWEED

B EN SPENDS A WEEK at the coast every summer with his family. While he's there, he gathers up five-gallon pails of seaweed from the beach. He gets a lot of weird looks, and people ask him, "Are you going to eat it?"

Well, not exactly. Not as seaweed, per se.

Back at the beach house, he hoses off the seaweed to de-salt it. By the end of the week he has three or five buckets full of seaweed, which he loads into trash bags and drives back to his mountain home.

Living in the mountains, Ben buys Ice Melt by the five-gallon bucket, so he has a good supply of buckets. He uses the salt in the winter to de-ice his sidewalk, and then, in the summer, he keeps de-salted seaweed from the beach in his buckets.

As a single person, Ben has a smallish compost heap, so he mixes the seaweed into the pile so that he doesn't overwhelm it. Seaweed qualifies as "green," so he layers it with brown leaves.

One great thing about seaweed—it doesn't have any weed seeds!

FISH POND ALGAE

O H, THOSE PHOTOS OF fish ponds in gardening books look so attractive but then, like every good thing, the pond is accompanied by trouble. The trouble with fish ponds is algae.

Algae grows when sunlight hits the water in the fish pond. The combination of sunlight, warm water, and nutrients in the water (e.g., fertilizer from the lawn and garden or the fish manure) contributes to algae growth. This disadvantage can be turned your advantage because algae is green and you can compost it. I always need more green in my compost pile, which is largely composed of yard and garden detritus.

Scoop the algae out of the pond with a rake, put it in a bucket, and carry it to the compost pile. Chances are the algae or the leaf sludge lying on the bottom of the fishpond will be smelly. Not to worry. Cleaning up the algae is a great opportunity to take away one of the competitors for the oxygen in the water. Your pond fish need oxygen just as you do. With the onset of winter and ice, the fishpond can become anaerobic due to the oxygen being used by decaying leaves.

THINGS THEY SAY
ARE COMPOSTABLE

Nowadays, all sorts of food containers say they are compostable. Bamboo plates, plastic cups made from corn, plastic bags made from cornstarch, paper plates made from sugar cane, plastic forks and spoons made from plant-based plastics.

I have thrown many of these into my compost pile with disappointing results. Now, I have to say, my compost pile does not get hot. I have six compost piles, but none of them are bigger than 3' x 3' x 3'. In other words, they are not big enough to get hot.

The bamboo plates took five years to disappear. When I uncovered a more-or-less whole cornstarch plastic bag, I just couldn't bear to wait another two years to find out whether it would actually compost. Into the trash it went. The plastic cups made from corn had shattered into slivers three years after I composted them, but did not look even slightly decomposed. Into the trash they went also.

So, for the home composter, I wouldn't advice adding these so-called "compostables" to your compost pile.

COMPOST TO THE BRIM

M Y COMPOST BIN IS full, and I'm still adding to it. Fortunately, every day it sinks an inch, like a freshly dug grave.

The compost pile I'm subtracting from is young. I can still see the remains of last summer's clean-up when I ripped out a sizable patch of pachysandra and yanked out galloping ostrich ferns. The rhizomes of both are still completely recognizable. Only the green leaves have decomposed and disappeared.

I sift the young compost through a screen and into a wheelbarrow and throw the chunky remains into the full compost pile. Every day I fill it to the brim. Every night, the heap sinks as if it's exhaling its last breath.

One of these days we too will be on the compost pile of life, with our cremains spread on land or water.

Until then, I'll enjoy the feel of the fresh, rich compost sifting through my fingers.

MONTH-BY-MONTH COMPOST

THE COMPOSITION OF MY compost pile varies from month to month. Here's a snapshot of what you're likely to find.

JANUARY

orange rinds from juice oranges

fruitcake or other uneaten Christmas baked goods

candy canes

paper-white Narcissus—bulbs and leaves

used Kleenexes

molded fiber "cardboard" (that holds new
electronic products)

rotten butternut squash

FEBRUARY

grapefruit rinds

compostable take-out "clamshell" container

2 hole-y wool socks

a pair of hole-y cotton underpants with stretched-
out elastic (I'll find the elastic band in a
couple of years, and throw it in the trash.)

MARCH

leaves

the last winter squash, which rotted when
   I wasn't looking

the Christmas wreath (I'll rescue the wreath ring
   when I happen it across it in a couple of years
   and use it again to make another wreath that
   December.)

APRIL

Easter candy

Easter eggshells

winter mulch

flowerbed clean-up

beech leaves (which finally fall off the trees)

MAY

ferns

Easter lily

JUNE

Johnny-jump-ups

potted pansies

Christmas cyclamen

JULY

grass clippings

Christmas poinsettia

AUGUST
dried-up poppy stems and pods
dried out money plant
zucchini (really big ones)
last year's garlic, which has either sprouted
    or dried up

SEPTEMBER
rotten tomatoes
tomato plants

OCTOBER
phlox stems
beebalm stems
frozen marigolds
other frosted annuals
leaves
broccoli stalks

NOVEMBER
jack-o-lantern
Halloween candy
some ashes from the wood stove (I didn't do it;
    my sweetie did!)
dead potted mums
cornstalks
kale ribs

DECEMBER

    1 hole-y wool sock
    a mouse-eaten woolen hat
    flimsy Chinese cardboard that the recycling
        center doesn't want
    walnut shells from the nutcracker in the house
    clementine peels
    frozen gourds
    turnip tops
    parsnip tops
    leek leaves
    Brussels sprout stalks

Inch by inch, month by month, this compost is going to make my garden grow.

THE REALITY
OF COMPOSTING

TIME FOR COMPOST

My neighbor complains that her compost pile barely produces any compost. She piles up all the brown stuff in the fall, and in the spring, it's still brown. After 45 minutes of sorting through all the phlox stems and squash vines from last year, she finally finds some compost—just enough to fill a wheelbarrow.

"Your compost looks so great," she tells me. "How do you do it?"

"Time" is my answer. The soil in my compost bin is rich and dark, there's plenty of it, and it's three years old. I build a compost pile and leave it alone for two or three years. I do not pull it apart the following spring. I am not tempted to just throw a handful of compost on top of an old bin.

This means I need three compost bins: one for this year, one for last year, and one for the year before that. The bin I'm using now was indeed put together three years ago; I know this because I just found the not-yet-decomposed bamboo paper plates from another neighbor's daughter's outdoor wedding three summers ago. I pitched those flimsy remains into the current "new" bin that I'm adding to. Maybe they'll finally be biodegraded the next time I see them, three years from now.

I am as busy in my life as the next person. I do not have the time, energy, or desire to turn compost, and neither do you. So don't give yourself a hard time about your pathetic compost pile. Instead of using your precious time for the care and feeding and turning of the compost pile, just let Nature take her time and do the work of composting for you.

POLITICALLY CORRECT COMPOST

I'M MASTER COMPOSTER, AND I wonder if this means my own compost should be P.C. Politically correct compost would not have any half-decayed woolen socks in it.

Since 1993, my approach to compost has been inspired by Vera Work, a social worker and Holocaust survivor, who offered a weekend workshop on Post-Traumatic Stress Disorder while I was studying to be a Mental Health Counselor at Antioch University New England. Vera brought in a jar of compost that included a large rusty nail, a bit of rag, and a chicken bone. The message for the traumatized client was clear: Everything eventually decomposes.

For years, I threw old ripped woolen or cotton shirts or sweaters—clothes that had no future even in a big yellow Planet Aid box—into my compost. I thought decrepit clothes could aid the soil of my garden instead.

But then, digging into a three-year-old compost bin, I'd shovel out a more or less whole green sweater matted with fibrous roots. Maybe it wasn't wool after all? A braided rug decayed into one- or two-foot lengths. I'd pull out the partial braids and snake them into the neighboring bin, where I'd run into the blue strands a year or two later. The leather remains of a moccasin from

Alaska lined with rabbit fur—I had worn holes in the sole at the heel and the ball of the foot. A shred of a filmy cotton blouse my mother gave me for Christmas in 1977 still floats around my vegetable garden.

Now, when I pull what remains of a leather glove or a hot pad out of the compost, I put it in the trash bag that's headed for the dumpster. I wonder what archaeologists a thousand years from now will make of a grimy, dirt laden, and ripped black cotton t-shirt?

Maybe I should stop throwing my ratty old clothes into the compost. I could toss a hole-y wool sock into the trash, toe the line, and keep politically correct compost. No clothes. Just naked compost.

TO TURN? OR NOT TO TURN?

B EN HAS ONE COMPOST pile out in the back corner of his yard—just a loose heap unconstrained by bins. Every couple of weeks, he takes ten minutes and turns the pile from right to left, layering as he goes. Two or four weeks later, when he's walking by with a shovel in his hand, he turns the pile from left to right. Basically, he's turning the pile upside down at least once a month.

The key to Ben's ease with turning is that he's not turning his pile in place. He has one compost pile, but two "compost spots," and he's moving his pile from one spot to the other.

Mary Lou gave up on turning her compost piles, because she didn't see that turning every three weeks hurried the process of decomposition.

Tatiana calls herself a lazy gardener when it comes to turning compost, but if you saw her tiny organic farm and her dozen compost bins, you would not call her lazy. "I only turn my compost once a year, in the spring," she says. No wonder.

Her definition of "turning" is taking the undecomposed top layer off the most mature pile, and throwing it back onto the resting pile or into an empty bin.

"Dig down until you get to the good stuff," she says.

Now it's your turn to decide: To turn? Or not to turn?

COMPOST EXERCISE ROUTINE

M AVIS, THE THINNEST WOMAN on the block, loves to go out and turn the compost piles in her community garden. She says that using the compost pile as your exercise is so rewarding, it's not a waste.

Her routine goes like this: The community garden has four bins, and gardeners always add to the bin closest to the garden. The instructions to the other gardeners are simple: Add to #1 and take compost from #4.

Meanwhile, Mavis-the-compost-maven is taking care of what's happening in the middle. In the spring, as soon as the compost thaws, Mavis forks #3 into #4.

Then she turns #2 into the now-emptied #3, and #1 into the now-emptied #2. As she is turning #1 into #2, she can layer and water as needed. If she runs into a batch of garbage, then she adds a layer of mulch hay or leaves. Then the first bin, the one closest to the plots, is empty again and ready to be filled up during the spring, summer, and fall.

And Mavis feels great!

LAZY AERATION

THE PURPOSE OF TURNING your compost pile is to aerate it and give the aerobic bacteria some breathing space, so they can get to work decomposing your compost. However, not all of us have the time or energy to turn our piles. Some gardeners have devised their own short-cut methods of aeration.

Tatiana starts her compost piles with a floor of brushy stuff, dead perennial stems, or cornstalks in order to help aeration. As she's building the pile, she sticks in four or five long vertical sticks; later she extracts the sticks, creating columns of air to help aeration.

Whit, who makes his bins from four pallets each, lays down a fifth pallet (perhaps an old rotting one) as the "floor." This floor pallet creates an airflow under the compost pile. This method is particularly useful if the ground is damp or the climate soggy. Aeration is quite helpful for compost piles with high moisture content, because it prevents odors.

A compost aerator is a tool that looks like a four-foot long corkscrew with a handle, which enables you to drill down into your compost pile and bring up material from the center of the pile. Using the aerator is a way to turn the pile without actually turning the pile, so it's much easier on your back.

Aerate your compost pile and create beautiful compost.

LEAF MOLD

O UR LOCAL GARDEN COLUMNIST, Henry Homeyer, wrote a few years ago about leaf mold as a soil conditioner, so I thought I'd try it. I made a cylinder of chicken wire, about four or five feet in diameter, so that I simply bent and hooked the end wires onto the beginning mesh. I staked it into the ground with some old broom handles and a couple of stray fence posts I happened to have.

That fall I filled the wired cylinder to the brim with leaves from the yard. Then I forgot about it for two years.

I recently looked at it, and, oh my, that humus is dark and beautiful. Four feet of leaves settled down into six inches of leaf mold.

If you pay more attention to your leaves than I did, you can make the leaves decompose faster. Watering them once a week prevents them from drying out, which would slow down the decomposition process.

If you feel energetic, you can line your enclosure with cardboard, which will help maintain dampness.

And if you feel really diligent you can shred the leaves with the lawn mower before dumping them into the wire cage. That way you can fit more in.

Or break the mold, and build a bin out of four pallets, and fill it up with leaves. A pallet bin and a four-foot-wide chicken-wire cylinder will each hold about 16 trash bags of leaves.

Turn over a new leaf, and use leaf mold for compost. Just leave that giant pile of leaves alone, and you can make leaf mold. If you leave the pile high and dry, it will take two years. You can take it or leave it, but leaf mold is good for your soil.

ROOT VEGETABLES AND
THE COMPOST SYSTEM

I ROASTED SOME ROOT VEGETABLES for dinner the other night. Everything from the garden: potatoes, onions, carrots, beets, garlic. By the time I finished peeling and chopping, slicing and dicing, I had two quarts of compost. (Carrot fronds take up a lot of space.)

I also wound up with about two quarts of dinner.

Out in the compost bin, I can almost see the pile compacting. The bin was totally full in July with fresh green pachysandra leaves; by September the pile has sunk and compacted, so that it's about a foot from the top of the bin. Every day I add another quart or two of kitchen waste, but at this rate, the bin never fills up.

Meanwhile, one of those two quarts of dinner is still in the refrigerator. The missing quart disappeared into our mouths and is wending its way through the digestive systems of my sweetie and me. This "compaction" process is much shorter—about twelve hours for him and 24 hours for me. The end product is almost unrecognizable, and it has a totally different name from "roasted roots" or "dinner," so I mostly fail to notice the relationship.

The fruits (or vegetables) of the earth go into my body via my mouth, are "composted" by the heat and metabolism of the body, and exit via the rear door. The "solid waste" returns to the earth from which it came via another circuitous route of pipes—toilet to PVC pipes to sewer (or septic tank in my case) to waste treatment (ahem) plant and then back into the streams and rivers of nature.

By this time, we've totally lost interest and thus fail to see the whole ecological cycle that binds us together with people downstream from us.

WINTER COMPOST

I F YOU'RE NOT KEEN on trudging out to the winter compost pile, then you can accumulate more compost before you trek out to the deep freeze of the great outdoors.

My compost bucket holds less than two quarts, so I have to walk to my compost pile at least once and usually twice a day. Fortunately, my compost pile is inches away from my driveway, so I have easy access, even in deep snow.

My neighbors keep a step-on trash can under their sink. Although this is very convenient, I do sometimes suspect the smell in their house emanates from their three-gallon collection of kitchen scraps.

Ben keeps a five-gallon bucket on his unheated back porch and collects his compost there. Then once a month, when the weather is good, he trudges out to his compost heap in the back yard. Yes, the compost is probably frozen into the bucket, but he simply turns the bucket upside down on the compost heap, and gives it a few good twhacks with a shovel until the giant compost ice cube falls out.

Barbara, who lives in town, keeps her compost in a small box in her car in the winter. Most nights, it freezes solid. Then when she happens to be driving by the landfill, she can deliver her frozen dinner leftovers to the composting program.

How close is your winter compost? Too close (in the kitchen)? Too far away (through the snowy yard or on the other side of town)? Or just right (beside the driveway)?

How often you need to go depends on whether you can hold it. But then, when you've gotta go, you've gotta go.

COMPOSTING IN THE WINTER

IT'S COLD OUTDOORS. YOU'RE cold. Your compost pile is cold. Probably frozen solid. At least you can move. But maybe you don't want to go to your compost. That nice summer stroll has turned into an icy winter trudge.

Maybe there's even a silent argument going on in your kitchen. "You take out the compost." "No, you." "No, you." Or maybe you're having the argument with yourself. "I should." "I don't want to."

You're snowed in. Your compost pile is snowed in.

It takes intention to brave the winter winds and walk out to the compost pile. Remember your intention. Why do you have a compost pile anyway?

If you didn't care, you would throw your kitchen scraps into the trash and forget about it. But you have second thoughts about that course of action. It just doesn't feel right.

You could think of your compost run as feeding the birds and the squirrels. You could think of your compost run as exercise and a bit of fresh air. You could think of it as feeding your garden.

But really, perhaps, when you take out the compost, you are feeding your soul.

SHE LOVES TO TAKE OUT THE COMPOST IN THE WINTER

DIANA LOVES TO TAKE out her kitchen compost bucket in the winter, even though she has to trek across a hundred feet of snow. While she walks, she is busy tracking: looking for the footprints of animals who have been visiting her lid-less black plastic composter.

She sees the blue jays fly away. She can hear the crows an hour after sunrise. But she is on the lookout for the calling cards of smaller visitors. Mouse tracks. Squirrels—both gray and red. Fox—both red and gray. Chipmunks in February and March. Turkeys, raccoons, rabbits, and deer. Once in a while, she is surprised by less common visitors.

Diana's neighbor, Lynn Levine, has written an easy and excellent guide: *Mammal Tracks and Scat* (www. heartwoodpress.com), which Diana can refer to if she has a question about who has left their footprint. She herself is so committed to leaving a smaller carbon footprint, that she doesn't mind tracking out to the winter compost.

120 DEGREES IN FEBRUARY

GREG, WHO LIVES IN town, has a sort of little car-port for his garden cart (a cart-port?) and his garden tools, and this is where he keeps his wide-mouthed black plastic composter. It happens to be on the south side of his garage, but he doesn't think the southern exposure has anything to do with how hot his compost gets.

The important thing is that the cart-port roof of corrugated fiberglass keeps the snow away from the com-poster. The second important thing is that every time he adds more kitchen scraps to his pile, he digs in a little bit with his pitchfork. So he's always putting his scraps in the middle of the pile, not just laying them on top.

Then in February, his pile is cooking, steaming at 120 degrees. His other compost pile, out in the yard, is sur-rounded by snow, and it's a block of ice that won't thaw until May.

Keeping the snow away from the pile is like taking the compost out of the deep freeze. Keeping the snow away from the compost pile makes all the difference, says Greg.

During the January thaw, he gathers some more dead leaves from the yard, so that when the next eight inches of snow arrives in February, he has some brown to mix in with the kitchen scraps, which are heating up and getting stinky. The leaves take the stink away.

Greg's compost is cooking in February and March and will be ready to serve up in the spring.

THAWING THE COMPOST PILE

I HAVE A CONFESSION TO make. I'm a Master Composter, it's early spring, and....

My compost pile is an iceberg.

Yes, I know the heap is supposed to be hot, but mine is cold. Really cold. Frozen solid. I managed to scrape two inches off the top before I hit the tundra.

This is just one more good reason to spread compost on the garden in November. Otherwise, when spring rolls around, and you're ready to use it, the compost pile is permafrost.

My iceberg compost reminds me of how I sometimes prepare dinner. At 5:00 P.M., I pull a container of food, or maybe a frozen chicken breast, out of the freezer. How am I going to work some magic on it so dinner will be ready by six?

Sometimes I microwave it, but sometimes I put it in a covered saucepan and slowly scrape the thawed part off, layer by layer, as if that will hurry it up. I'm not going to microwave the compost, nor am I going to take an ice ax to it. I just have to wait for the sun to add the heat.

So now it's time to practice patience. I know the snowbank on the north side of the house sometimes doesn't totally melt until early May. But it does melt.

And my compost will thaw out too. Firing up my internal impatience thermometer heats me up but does nothing to thaw the compost. So chill out, my friend. The warmth of spring is coming.

YOUNG COMPOST

L AST SPRING AND SUMMER, I used all my compost—five bins of it. Fortunately fall clean-up provided an excellent opportunity to fill up the bins, and I topped off each one with a thick layer of manure from a nearby farm.

This spring, I have young compost—all gangly with stems and undecomposed flotsam. So I'm screening my compost by using a flat (tray) and shaking it over the wheelbarrow. I particularly like a flat that has solid sides and holes that are not too big. Shake, shake, shake. Then I throw the oversized debris into the newest compost bin. The screened compost in the wheelbarrow, which I use for potting up plants to give away, is really beautiful.

RECYCLING THE CYCLE OF LIFE

I'M LOOKING FORWARD TO reaching the bottom of the compost pile I'm using. I can see part of the black plastic I laid down as the floor of the bin to keep the tree roots from growing into the bottom of the pile.

Every day I fill the wheelbarrow with lovely sifted and screened compost that looks rich and delicious. Every day I pot up two or three dozen plants for the Plant Sale at the library on Memorial Day weekend. One day I haul a truckload of plants to the library. The next day, I take another truckload.

Donating plants gives me a delicious satisfaction:

- I'm dividing plants in my garden and giving away the extras—it feels like spring house cleaning.

- I pot the extras up with free recycled pots from the Saturday Swap Program at the landfill.

- I'm using my own recycled compost that I know will give the plant a good start in its new home.

Recycling the cycle of life: plants to compost to plants.

DONE!

I REACHED THE BOTTOM OF one compost pile. Oh, how wonderful to finally see that black plastic "floor" and sweep it clean. I put the "gate" (the fourth pallet) back on that bin and immediately began filling it up again. The following Sunday, my gardening friend Melissa and I hauled two garden cart loads of lamium to that bin, filling it up about one-third of the way.

I begin sifting and screening my way through the middle bin, using the compost to pot up plants I've thinned out of my flower beds.

I feel a certain sense of accomplishment when I finish a project—or finish a compost bin. *There. That's done.* But I could just as well say, "It's gone." That compost pile is gone. The other thing that's gone is my desire to finish, to accomplish that particular thing. Desire has evaporated, and it feels <u>so</u> good to be desireless for a moment.

So what do I do? Start all over again. New compost pile. New desire. New wanting-to-finish. New stress, mild though it may be.

Simply recognize stress, in all its disguises. Recognize the truth of life.

SUMMER SOLSTICE BONFIRE

I BOUGHT AN ORGANIC CHICKEN at the Farmers'
Market and boiled it up to make chicken soup and
chicken salad. But what to do with the skin and bones?
You're not supposed to compost them, though my compost is full of chicken bones and spare ribs. I suppose they
add a slow-release calcium to the garden. Sometimes, I
stick a chicken bone next to a fledgling tomato plant in
hopes of a transfer of calcium.

In the winter, I cremate the bones in my wood stove.
But how to dispose of meat bones during the summer?
Surely, there's a biodegradable alternative to the trash.

On the summer solstice, I have a bone-fire. Yes, that's
where the word bonfire comes from—burning piles of
animal bones to make lime to sweeten the soil. I burn my
chicken bones, then sprinkle the cinders (slow-release
charcoal) and ashes from the bonfire on the lawn.

Celebrate the summer solstice with a bonfire before
the long summer days slowly burn shorter.

CRITTERS

CRITTER FEEDER

YES, CRITTERS COME TO my compost pile. I see chipmunks and blue jays picking their way through it in the morning, and I'm sure raccoons come at night, because someone is licking the eggshells clean.

One May morning, I saw a red squirrel jump out of the compost bin and onto a nearby pine tree with an avocado shell in its mouth. Up the tree it dashed, leaving me with the image of a red squirrel in a sombrero eating guacamole and chittering "Ai-yi-yi-yi."

You could think of your compost pile as a big, perhaps somewhat unsightly, bird feeder or squirrel feeder. Cute. But when it comes to bigger critters, you or your neighbors may have some concerns. You really don't want a neighborhood dog pawing through the remains of last night's dinner. And you do not want to attract bears. As to the mid-sized mammals that are happy to dine at the buffet table of the compost pile for their own moonlight dinner, well, that's your decision.

Fear of critters is the number one reason why people decide not to compost. But there are ways around this issue. Simply do not compost your kitchen waste. You can still run it through the garbage disposal and send all those nutrients downstream. You could bury it eight inches deep in the garden. Or you could bring some creatures indoors, and compost using red worms in a Rubbermaid tub.

Your compost is someone's dinner in disguise. Who will it be?

STINKY THOUGHTS

ONE SPRING EVENING AT 9 P.M., I made my final run to the compost pile and accidentally beaned a skunk on the nose with a watermelon rind. I didn't stick around for a closer sighting, once I saw that furry white tail start to twitch. When my sweetie came home fifteen minutes later, he said he smelled skunk.

Our thoughts and actions go into a "compost pile" from moment to moment. A thought arises; then it passes. A deed happens; then it's over. Even though it's gone, it leaves the track of its valence. A wholesome thought or deed—of kindness or generosity—lays the path for more wholesome thoughts and deeds. An unwholesome thought or deed lays the pathway for more of the same. In the language of neuroscience, "Neurons that fire together, wire together." In the language of gardeners, "You reap what you sow."

So be careful what you compost. Those stinky thoughts may come back to haunt you.

DEFENDING YOUR COMPOST

T HE NUMBER ONE REASON why people don't compost is fear of varmints.

Predator pets—such as a dog or a cat—that spend time outdoors are your first line of defense against the four-legged critters you don't want raiding your compost. The pet patrol can be very effective at keeping bandits at bay. Cats will crouch nearby for hours, staking out the compost pile for little furry tidbits.

Your pets may never actually take the varmints into custody. Just the smell of carnivore poop and pee can be enough to deter visits from bothersome herbivores who would otherwise find a compost pile to be a handy grocery store. However, you do not want your pets to cross the line and get into the compost themselves. You may have to arrest your dog's tendency to joyfully leap into the bin for a snack. You especially do <u>not</u> want pet poop in your compost.

If your pets abide by the rules you set, they will defend your compost pile against raiders of every stripe.

DANCING RACCOONS

AT MY ANNUAL MONTH-LONG meditation retreat, my daily chore was to take out the trash, the
compost, and the recycling. What a perfect job for this
Master Composter!

As I walked out the kitchen door with a five-gallon
bucket of kitchen waste, I would sometimes be met by a
dancing raccoon that wanted what was in the bucket but
was too shy to come too close. As I crossed the driveway,
the mother raccoon and her youngun disappeared into a
bamboo grove. Meanwhile, ahead of me, I could see two
raccoons coming out of the woods, scurrying toward the
large compost pile of the retreat center.

The retreat center had three large compost bins next
to each other. Each one was six feet long and six feet
wide. The finished one had sunk down to about four feet
tall. I dumped my haul into the middle one, which was of
equal height and had about two feet more to go before it
reached the brim.

Every morning there was enough oatmeal in the
bucket to feed five people. The queen raccoon straddled
this and hissed at the others to shoo them away. The raccoons didn't care about cucumbers and carrot peelings,
but they did love toast and apple cores. Tea bags and coffee grounds were just an occupational hazard. The lowest

raccoon on the totem pole grabbed half a banana and scurried a few feet away to keep his bounty to himself.

Raccoon scat can contain giardia and roundworms, so we definitely do not want raccoons eating in our compost and then relieving themselves on the poop deck, so to speak. If raccoons are visiting your compost, you can put your kitchen scraps in a blender, add water, and grind them to a slurry. Or you can put the scraps into the middle of the pile. Or you can turn the pile frequently. Or give your scraps to your neighborhood chickens, and let them recycle your dinner.

COMPOSTING WITH BEARS

BEN, WHO LIVES UP in the mountains on the edge of a National Forest, has bears for neighbors, yet he still builds a compost pile, and the bears do not bother it. He definitely does not add any meat or dairy to his pile. When he does take out his compost bucket, he buries the kitchen scraps in the middle of the pile, so they are well camouflaged.

In addition to never adding meat, fish, or dairy products, Ben also does not add oil, un-rinsed eggshells, cooked food, or large amounts of fruit. These food scraps will attract bears long before they decompose.

In the winter, when the bears are hibernating, Ben's pile is frozen, of course, so he just dumps his compost bucket on top of the pile.

Ben enjoys turning his compost pile, and this is one of the keys to keeping bears out of the compost bin.

BEARS IN THE NEIGHBORHOOD

After 30 years, a bear found and destroyed my neighbor's black plastic compost bin. Here in our yard, we found three piles of bear scat, but our open compost piles were not touched. Another neighbor saw a bear as she was taking a walk in the woods around dusk—a small bear, she said.

As cute as they are, we are talking about a life and death situation—for the bear. If a bear becomes habituated to people food, then the game warden will be called to "remove" it.

Several of my neighbors are taking these bear sightings seriously. Lynn and Cliff, the 30-year veteran composters, are now taking their kitchen scraps to another neighbor's chickens. The owner of the chickens likes this solution because it means she has to buy less feed for her free-ranging chickens that roam her yard.

Lynn and Cliff's garbage is now composted by chickens. Garbage in; chicken manure out—also eggs. Lynn and Cliff now receive free eggs in exchange for feeding the chickens.

In this reorganizing of neighborhood composting, the chickens win. Their owner wins. Lynn and Cliff win. And now that the temptation has been removed, even though the bear has lost a free and easy lunch, the bear has won its life.

USING YOUR COMPOST

COMPOST TEA

I F COMPOST IS YOUR cup of tea, then pour a little compost tea on your plants. Brew some brown "tea" for your garden plants by filling a five-gallon bucket about half full of compost. Then top it off with water from the garden hose, or just let the next rainstorm fill up the bucket for you.

Let your compost tea steep for several days.

If you have placed your compost bucket / "teapot" near where you will be using it, you can simply pour the "tea" onto nearby plants. Otherwise, you might ladle the compost tea into a smaller bucket. Don't use a watering can because bits of compost will clog the watering holes.

You can fill the bucket with water again and make another pot of compost tea. Your second "pot" will be weaker than the first, but still nourishing. Convert the second batch into high tea by feeding your plants the compost dregs that remain in the bucket, and your plants will grow higher still.

SIFTING COMPOST

M ARY LOU HAS A clinker sifter that her father gave her decades ago. Back in the days of coal furnaces, a clinker sifter was used to sift the coal ashes and then throw the bigger, usable bits of coal back into the stove. The round sifter, about a foot in diameter, has a screen with half-inch mesh.

Mary Lou uses the big flat sieve to sift her finished compost. The rather large mesh holes enable small clods of compost to fall through to the five-gallon bucket sitting underneath. She sifts out stalks and stems and rocks and throws the uncomposted bits back into the "unfinished" compost pile.

I use a flat or plant tray that has solid sides and big-enough—but not too big—holes in the bottom. I fill the tray with compost and jiggle it over the wheelbarrow.

Mary Lou uses her sifted compost to fill old window boxes. Because compost has a tendency to be dry, she saturates the window boxes with water for a couple of days. Then she seeds them with lettuce, spinach, and arugula in April and again in August. She sets her window boxes in her ratty old greenhouse, where she does have to water the greens in her window boxes every day. She transplants the seedlings into her garden, and harvests fresh greens from April through June and again from August through October.

After sifting through all this advice about your compost, you could buy a fancy sifter from the gardening catalog, but you can just as well make do with hardware cloth, deer fencing, or a hole-y plant tray as your compost sifter…if you even sift at all.

RECIPE FOR POTTING SOIL

I HAVE NOT YET FOUND the perfect potting soil in a bag. I buy the cheap stuff; I buy the expensive stuff. I buy the organic stuff. Sigh.

Potting soil ranges from heavy on the peat moss to heavy on the sand to something that looks like not-yet-decomposed bark mulch. Then there's the potting mix that does look like dirt, which still has little sticks and rocks in it. Potting soil seldom uses actual soil, because soil is considered too heavy for houseplants. So all the potting soil we buy is actually soil-less.

I've had enough experience with so-called potting soils to know that some "soil" dries out completely within a day or two.

What do you do when faced with dry skin? Use a moisturizer. The moisturizers for our potting soil are per-lite or vermiculite, naturally occurring silicates (sand), which hold water.

You can double the volume and fertility of your potting soil by expanding it with your homemade compost. Mix:

1 cup potting soil
1 cup compost
2/3 cup vermiculite or perlite

Adding compost to your potting soil not only boosts the growth of your houseplants; it inoculates them against diseases with some good bacteria.

The potting soil you buy is sterilized. You can bake your own potting soil, if you want to, but baking kills not only the bad bacteria, but also the good, sort of like antibiotics do in the body. Compost is probiotic for your houseplants.

One more advantage of using compost in your potting soil: you'll be growing the flowers and vegetables you threw into your compost! Last winter I found cherry tomatoes growing in three houseplants. They were spindly, but I did like picking a fresh cherry tomato right off the vine in March.

POOPETS

At a Farmers' Market, I found a vendor selling poopets. These are "pets" made from poop. Cow or horse manure is sculpted into dung bunnies, stool pigeons, and turdles. I put a stool toad in my three-feet-tall banana tree at Christmas, and by May, the tree had grown to five feet. The toad poopet slowly dissolved into a lump, recognizable as a toad only to me.

These poopets are completely odorless. They are definitely organic, and they slowly release nutrients into your potted plants every time you water. Or scatter them around the plants in your garden and let the rain wash their organic fertilizer into the soil.

You can make your own poopets by using aged manure that has lost its smell. Horse manure is great because a horse only digests 20 percent of the grass it eats. As a result, horse droppings have a lot of fiber, which serves to hold the mixture together. If you're using plain cow manure, you might add a few grass clippings if the manure is not already mixed up with bedding straw.

Add water to the odorless manure to create a slurry, and let it dry for a week, until it's the texture of adobe. Then put your manure-clay in a plastic mold. Set your molded "pet" out in the sun to dry.

For the pooped-out potting soil in your houseplants, poopets are a fun way to add compost.

COMPOST GROWS
IN THE GARDEN

KAY IS THE GARDENER of her family, but in April she asked her husband Tom to put the compost on the garden. He spread the entire contents of the black bin over the garden; then he rototilled.

By June, Kay was finding dozens of tomato plants sprouting in her garden, along with a couple of peppers, an unknown squash (oh-oh), an avocado tree, and maybe a watermelon? For Kay, tomato plants were a weed; she pulled them out wholesale, except in certain spots, such as where the spinach didn't show up. She might as well have something growing there.

Pulling weeds, she came up with a lobster claw, lots of eggshells, and an interesting chunk of wet soil that turned out to be a rotten grape.

Burying your kitchen scraps in your garden, usually in a trench that is a foot or two deep in a currently unused section of the garden, is one form of composting.

The time to spread unfinished compost on the garden is in the fall. In our small compost piles at home, our winter compost is mostly going to just freeze and thaw anyway. By spreading it on the garden in November, you'll give it time to break down over the winter, and increase the humus of your garden.

GARDEN SURPRISES

I T'S A GOOD THING I like surprises.

Last spring I took buckets of compost to my community garden plot. I planted only winter squash and onions there, since I figured they wouldn't need much care, and I only go to the community garden once a week.

By July, I had a forest of tomatillos growing among the squash. That didn't surprise me. My compost has jillions of tomatillo seeds.

Meanwhile, most of the "weeds" that were growing in my onions were flowers. I dug out eight dozen *Nicotiana* (flowering tobacco) and one dozen *Verbascum* (a sweet perennial mullein that is only two feet tall.) I didn't have the heart to weed out *Cleome* (spider flower), *Nigella* (love-in-a-mist), Chinese forget-me-not (*Cynoglossum*), or the opium poppy (*Papaver somniflorum*) that blooms in late June. Trying to have both flowers and onions was counter-productive, so I had to separate them like rambunctious children.

In September, I harvested three winter squash, bushels of tomatillos, and growing right beside the garden gate, ground cherries! Also called Cape gooseberries, these little yellow-orange globes combine the sweetness and size of berries with a hint of tangy tomato-pineapple. Hiding in a paper husk, these little treasures love the heat of summer. I offered these surprises-from-the-compost to my community garden mates and watched them smile at the surprising taste and gift of little berries so late in the growing season.

In October, it was time to pull out the tomatillo bushes, the squash vines, and all the dead flowers, and put them in the compost bin. Perhaps you have a pretty good guess as to what I'm going to find growing in my vegetable garden next summer.

Your compost may have all sorts of surprises in store for you.

LASAGNA GARDENING

FOR ME LASAGNA GARDENING starts in April, but really, you can just begin when you begin.

If you're starting a garden from scratch, building the lasagna (cardboard, mulch hay, peat moss, compost, etc.) right on top of the turf is a lot of fun. I particularly like to do this in the fall, let it compost on the spot over the winter, and by spring, you are ready to dig in to dark, rich soil.

For my established flowerbeds, lasagna gardening begins in the spring, when the beds are littered with old leaves. Leave them in place. They are the first lasagna layer. I used to add a layer of bunny manure, and then a layer of bark mulch. You could add a layer of compost, and then bark mulch. Now I add a special mix of bark mulch that has well-composted manure already in it. Voila! The finished gardens look great.

For the vegetable garden, I pile on mulch hay in the fall, along with some wood ashes. If I'm really ambitious, I add a truckload of manure, either on top or underneath. In the spring, I pile on the compost.

In one of my flowerbeds, which is on a hillside and difficult to access, the lasagna starts in the fall when I cut down the brown stems of phlox and beebalm and simply leave them where they fall.

If it's brown,
cut it down.
If it's green,
it's clean.

This is the first lasagna layer. Leaves fall off the trees—second layer of lasagna. Come spring, mulch is thrown on the hillside—the third and final lasagna layer. By this time, the hillside looks tame. Only you and I know what's hiding underneath.

END OF GARDENING SEASON

WHEN THE GROWING SEASON is over, but you still have a little let's-go-outdoors-and-garden energy, while you're twiddling your green thumbs, use the last of the thin fall daylight to sprinkle or shovel compost onto your flowerbeds.

November is a good time to get a head start on spring. In the spring, the garden becomes a hive of activity. It's good to do as many of those spring chores as possible in late fall, sort of like prepping for a big dinner party by doing some things days (or, in this case, months) ahead.

Go ahead and use up all the compost you have. Compost, unlike a savings account, doesn't accrue interest in the bin. The return on your investment comes from spreading it around on your flower or vegetable gardens. And a good time to do that is when the plants are falling asleep for the winter.

Yes, it's chilly outdoors, but you'll warm up quickly by exercising those big muscle groups. Even if your compost isn't warm, you will be.

When I come indoors on a fall afternoon, in my dirty garden clothes, my sweetie hugs me and says, "You smell good. You smell like the outdoors."

Your compost smells and feels like delicious earth. And you are wearing the fragrance of happiness.

THE PHILOSOPHY OF COMPOSTING

HARVEST:
BOUNTY OR COMPOST?

I N THE HARVEST SEASON, I try to cook two or three vegetables from the garden for dinner every evening—broccoli or zucchini, chard or kale, and a salad made entirely of tomatoes. I leave the leftovers in the fridge for my sweetie. When I return from a long weekend away, they're still there.

"You're supposed to have eaten these," I say, with one eye on the overflowing harvest basket I just brought in from the vegetable garden.

"Oh, I did," he says. "Except for that yellow squash. You deal with that."

This is when the bounty of the garden takes a dive into exasperation. Too much of a good thing leads to some form of stress or other. There's nothing to do but throw the week-old leftovers into the compost. Then I spend an hour after dinner slicing tomatoes for the food drier or blanching broccoli for the freezer.

For years, after reading *The Magic of Findhorn*, I worried that the tomato devas might have their feelings hurt by wasting the food they guarded into fruition. But lately, I've come to see that waste is waste—whether it goes through my digestive system or straight into the compost pile.

And the great thing about waste—human, animal, or compost—is that you can use it grow more vegetables. Humanure, moo doo, zoo doo, or leftovers—it's not being wasted. It's all just compost.

RED RUSSIAN KALE

RUSSIAN RED KALE EASILY survives our New England winters, so, in early April, I harvest enough for dinner. Braised with onions and garlic from last summer's garden, our supper costs $0.

Two years ago, dinner leftovers went into the compost pile to become last spring's compost, which was spread on the vegetable garden to grow the kale and onions that we eat for dinner tonight. Any leftovers or onion skins go into the compost bucket and....

Kale—an exemplar of the circle of life that flows through us.

FUNERAL FLOWERS

I LIKE TO SEND FLOWERS to the family when someone dies, even though the obituary says "…in lieu of
flowers." Since I like flowers and I like to receive flowers,
I just assume other people do too. I often send the flowers
directly to the home rather than the funeral home.

In order to support local businesses, I go to
whitepages.com and type in "florist" and the zip code
where my friend lives. Then I call and order cut flowers
rather than an arrangement. Doesn't everyone already
have enough vases at home? I assume my friends do not
need another vase.

Funeral flowers remind us of the impermanence of
life. One day, one year, we are in full bloom. A few days
or decades later, we start to wilt. And finally death and
the compost pile.

Flowers don't have person-hood, so we can easily see
how decaying compost gives rise to new life. When it
comes to people, though, our attachment to person-hood
and to self interferes with this simple, straight-forward
understanding of nature.

A friend who had a heart attack and a near-death
experience said she looked down at the carcass on the
table—the carcass she had formerly called her "self."

Really, how are our physical bodies really any different from flowers?

JOHNNY-JUMP-UPS
AS A COVER CROP

THE PURPOSE OF A cover crop is to increase fertility of the soil, to decrease weeds and pests, and to create biodiversity. Cover crops are called green manure because farmers plow these nitrogen-rich crops into the ground where they improve the soil.

Most cover crops are in the legume family (alfalfa, vetch, clover) or in the grasses family (rye, oats, wheat, buckwheat), but they also include mustard and arugula of the *Brassica* family.

Every spring, my vegetable garden and the nearby strip beds are covered in Johnny-jump-ups (Jjus). They're cute, and to me, they're a weed. But now, I've decided I'm using Johnny-jump-ups as my cover crop. Here's why:

- Jjus don't prevent weeds exactly, but each plant covers half a square foot, and nothing grows in the shade of a Jju.
- They bloom profusely in April and May and are a joy to behold.
- In late June, they become leggy, so I pull them out wholesale and fill one compost bin completely full

of Jjus. Although they don't fix nitrogen, they add "green" manure to my compost bins.

Too many Johnny-jump-ups are a win-win situation. Beautiful flowering beds in April and May, and an overflowing green compost bin in June to really get that compost working.

THE LIVING DEAD

ALTHOUGH WE TYPICALLY THINK of our compost pile as composed of dead matter, this is not quite true. A dead tree, for instance, is home to 52 species of creatures. And our compost heap is also home to many living creatures, some so small we cannot see them.

Into the compost pile go dead plants and dead leaves, along with rotting fruits and vegetables that have overstayed their welcome in our refrigerator. What we usually call "dead" is precious life for someone, something else.

Little mites, sow bugs, centipedes, and various larvae come to feast and thereby hasten the process of decomposing. Nematodes, mitochondria, and other invisible bacteria and microbes are also at work, converting death into life.

When you open your black plastic composting unit in the spring, stand aside for a minute and let life fly out. Then carry your living compost to your garden, and let life begin to feed the new growth of seedlings and plants.

It's a miracle, isn't it? Life springs from all those dead marigolds, dead and rotting vegetables, and dead houseplants. It's enough to give us hope.

ACKNOWLEDGMENTS

THANKS TO MY FELLOW Master Gardeners and Master Composters who told me their compost stories: Greg Howe, Steve Squires, Tatiana Schreiber of Sowing Peace Farm, Cass Morgan, Ben St. George, and Mary Lou Buchanan. My neighbors are a constant source of compost questions: Connie Woodberry, Diana Wahle, John Warren, Lynn Levine, Cliff Adler, and Whit Wheeler.

Susan Pollack, editor, always gives me down-to-earth advice about structure. She takes the detours out of my writing and develops a straight path for the reader to follow. Kudos to proof-reader extraordinaire, Jenny Holan, who scrubs my manuscript clean. Oh! Does that feel good. Book designer Carolyn Kasper creates my beautiful self-published books, which look professionally done. (They Are!) Thanks to pun-master David Hoitt for the title.

This collection of essays began as a lark when publisher Dede Cummings asked me to write some sidebars for her book on organic composting. Once I got started writing about compost, I couldn't stop. Thirty-four of these essays were previously published in *The Organic Composting Handbook: Simple Composting Techniques for a Healthy, Abundant Garden* by Dede Cummings (Skyhorse Publishing, 2015).